P.S. - you're invited ...

P.S.- you're invited...

40+ DIY Projects for All of Your
Fashion, Home Décor & Entertaining Needs

Erica Domesek

ATRIA BOOKS

NEW YORK LONDON TORONTO SYDNEY NEW DELHI

ATRIA BOOKS

A Division of Simon & Schuster, Inc.
1230 Avenue of the Americas
New York, NY 10020

Copyright © 2013 by ELD Creative, Inc.

First Atria Books hardcover edition September 2013

ATRIA BOOKS and colophon are trademarks of Simon & Schuster, Inc.

For information about special discounts for bulk purchases, please contact Simon & Schuster Special Sales at 1-866-506-1949 or business@simonandschuster.com.

The Simon & Schuster Speakers Bureau can bring authors to your live event. For more information or to book an event, contact the Simon & Schuster Speakers Bureau at 1-866-248-3049 or visit our website at www.simonspeakers.com.

Designed by Amy Risley

Editorial photography and image of Erica Domesek on page xiii by Michael Fine / michaelfinephotography.com

Illustrations by Erica Domesek

Photo on page xii by Jake Rosenberg for The Coveteur / thecoveteur.com

Manufactured in the United States of America

10 9 8 7 6 5 4 3 2

Library of Congress Cataloging-in-Publication data is available.

ISBN 978-1-4516-9859-6
ISBN 978-1-4516-9860-2 (ebook)

for jax —
you had me at batik...

CONTENTS

VIDEO INDEX

ATRIA SMART BOOK
READ • WATCH • LISTEN • LEARN

P.S.- ▶ this...
HOW-TO VIDEO

Look for this video prompt throughout the book to access ENHANCED DIGITAL CONTENT. Simply download the FREE APP at gettag.mobi, hold your phone's camera a few inches away from the tag, and discover exclusive TIPS, HINTS & TIDBITS from Erica.

You can also visit pages.simonandschuster.com/PSYoureInvited to access the videos.
P.S. - If you access content through a mobile device, message and data rates may apply.

FRINGE GARLAND

page 5

PEARL CHANDELIER

page 19

PATCHWORK BLANKET

page 33

GLITTER COASTERS

page 57

WATERMELON POP

STRIPED CHAMPAGNE FLUTES

DOTTED TABLE EDGE

*MERCURY GLASS
CANDLESTICK HOLDERS*

DIP-DYE RUGS

*GOLDEN TREE
STUMP SIDE TABLE*

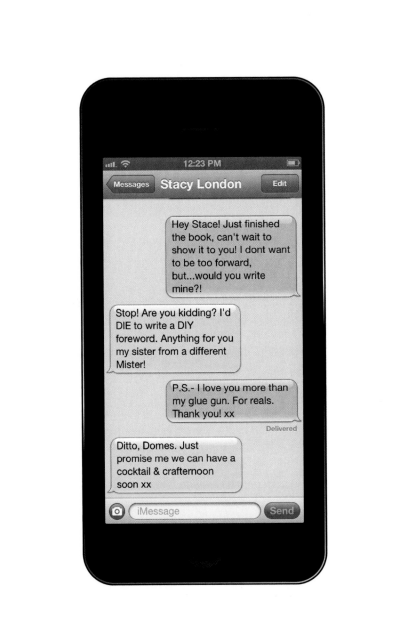

FOREWORD

For as long as I can remember, I always thought *do it yourself* was a phrase related to construction and home improvement . . . the types of things carpenters do, so I associated it with Home Depot aisles filled with wood planks, paint cans, and WD-40.

The closest I've come to crafting has been on my TV show, TLC's *What Not to Wear,* on which I've encountered many a crappy macramé tank top that should have been a plant holder in the first place.

That was until I met Erica: a supercool, ultrastylish, unpretentious vixen who changed my perception of DIY and crafting forever. With her infectious enthusiasm and endless patience, Erica taught me to see mundane objects as something new: an endless world of beautiful possibilities.

Whatever you think you know about crafting, this chick has already thought of it, perfected it into something entirely new and modern and, most important, something we can do, too. What I love and admire most about her and her mission is that she provides so much inspiration and motivation to create, and make our lives as lovely, colorful, vibrant, and original as whatever we can dream up.

Make glitter coasters out of cardboard? Hell, YEAH. A striped wineglass with nail polish? DUH. A side table from a tree trunk? NATCH. All we have to do is take what is right in front of us, what we already have at home, and enhance it, imagine a whole new life for it, and HAVE FUN.

When Erica says "P.S.- you're invited . . . ," it's a party from which you'll never go home empty-handed.

Stay crafty,*
Stacy London

*. . . P.S.- I stole that.

INTRODUCTION

Life is one gigantic DIY project that is constantly evolving, just like our own personal style. The most exciting thing about life is that it's all yours to design. I take an incredible amount of joy in discovering the road map to my happiness through creativity. My "I see it. I like it. I make it." mantra encourages me to embrace each day and live a more beautiful life by diving into DIY. This hands-on approach has always been my motivation in celebrating life and delivering smiles . . . which to me is the greatest accomplishment.

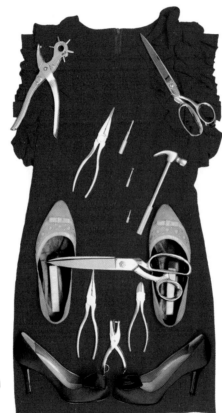

It all begins with a little inspiration. Everywhere I go, I'm always snapping pictures of anything and everything that makes me swoon and brings out my inner muse. Those shiny moments become the celebrations and everyday moments that are to D-I-Y for! After all, there's nothing I love more than creating special memories with friends and family that get dreamt up in my heart and executed with my hands.

My advice is simple: Don't wait for a get-together to get it together. You have every reason right in this book to comb for inspiration and start designing daily decadence for the everyday occasion that is life.

Take a minute to reflect on who you are today and what you want to create tomorrow, whether it's to display, wear, or share. Celebrate YOU from head to toe and every place you go. Use this book as your guide as you invite loved ones into the spectacular moments you take pride in designing, sharing, and celebrating. Dream up divine dinner parties, brightly colored birthday parties, a girls' game night, or an out-of-this-world outdoor fête. These extraordinary moments add layers of excitement and color to everything and everyone around you, so take note and get your glue gun ready as you start designing chic memories.

P.S.- It's easier than you think! Discovering everyday elements around the house to reuse, repurpose, and reimagine is as much a part of the creative process as dreaming up the projects themselves. Chances

are, you probably have hundreds of items around the house that are screaming for a reinvention.

Mark your RSVP "YES" to this invitation to live a more creative, imaginative, and beautiful life. Inspiration starts with the letter *i*, so don't wait for anyone else to rev up your creative engines. Be the driving force behind unforgettable moments that will make you proud to say "P.S.- I made this."

xo

stay crafty,

Erica

or as some of you know me . . .
@psimadethis

welcome to the craft closet...

paintbrushes
fabric paint
STRING
SPRAY PAINT
crystal trim

duct tape
glitter spray
fabric spray
PAPER TAPE
FABRIC DYE

GLUE
raffia
fabric
glitter

ZIPPERS

PUFFY PAINT

wooden beads

rubber bands

NAIL POLISH

ribbon

chain

embroidery thread

flat back gems

STUDS

BUTTONS

vintage charms

crystal beads

pom-pom trim

FEATHERS

SHELLS

markers

SAFETY PINS

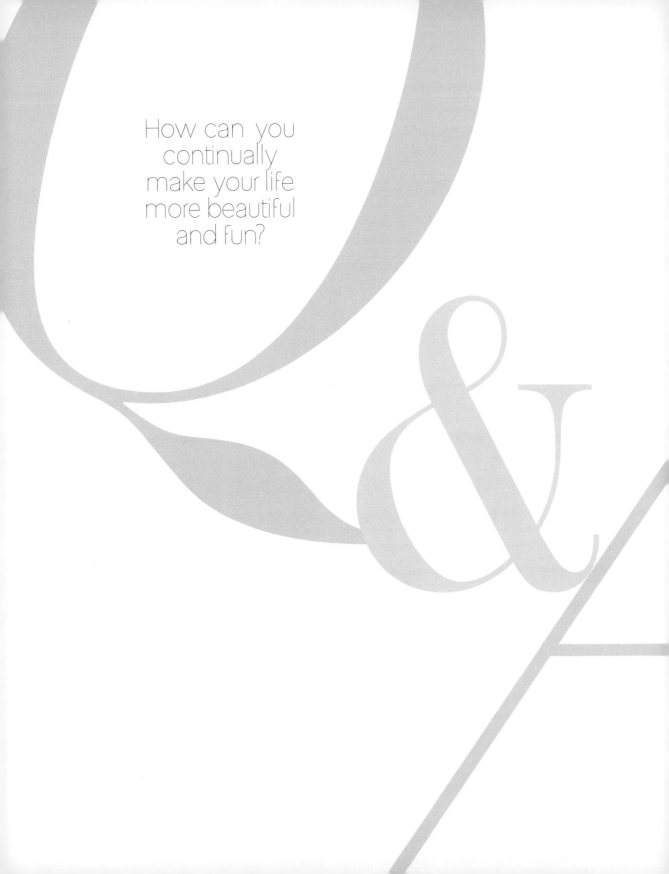

How can you
continually
make your life
more beautiful
and fun?

You simply...

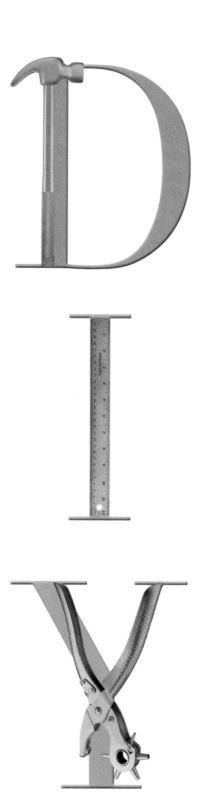

uno, dos, tres...
create a

festive
space

¡SEXY MEXI!

Crank up the heat from mild to medium until you reach hot hot hot at your next fiesta. Don't wait until Cinco de Mayo rolls around to be a señorita with a margarita. A sassy *mexicana* mama knows that more is more when you want to spice things up. Dashes of bold and lively colors infused into every detail down to decorative table accents and festive accessories are *muy necesarios*. Don't be afraid to introduce extra flavor into your world: you were born to repurpose everyday materials for dreamy DIYs. Reach for rope, raffia, and ribbon, and start creating vivid necklaces, garlands, vases, and purses that you'll savor forever.

1 | Fringe Garland

2 | Pom-pom Purse

3 | Fiesta Vases

4 | Knotted Tassel Necklace

FRINGE GARLAND

INGREDIENTS

- rope in multiple colors
- long strand of rope for base
- scissors

P.S.-Don't cut the base string until you're ready to hang the finished product!

Cut rope into 18-inch pieces, then fold in half and place each piece over long base string.

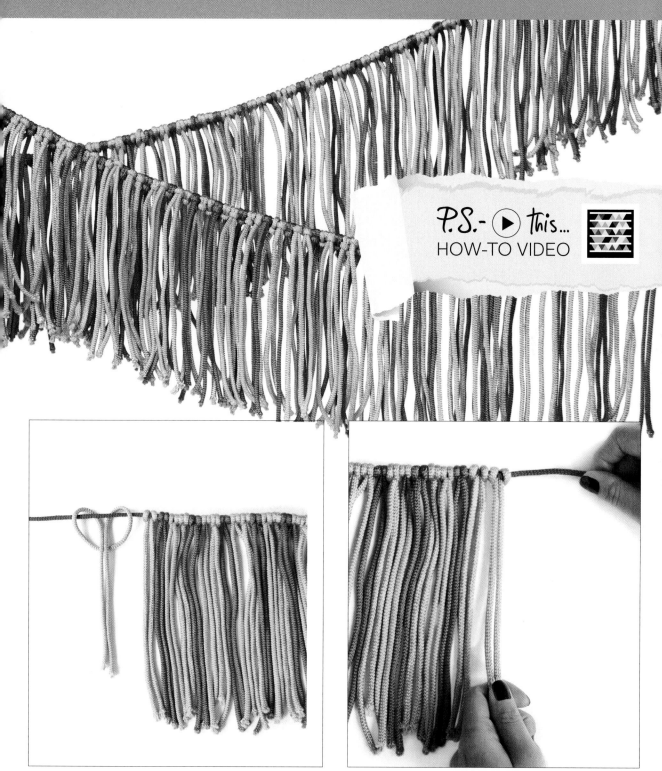

P.S.- ▶ this...
HOW-TO VIDEO

Loop around base string and pull through loop.

Pull tight and continue to fringe on!

P.S.-
POM-POM
PURSE

INGREDIENTS

- tote bag
- pom-pom trim
- variety of cloth ribbon
- fabric glue
- scissors

bag = bolsa

scissors = tijeras

crafty = creativa

Glue the reverse of pom-pom trim and press onto bag in a straight line. Hold in place for a few seconds until set.

Alternate trim and ribbons along the front, and continue to glue and wrap around back.

Keep going . . . cha cha cha . . .

Cut off any excess trim and ribbon.

P.S.-
FIESTA
VASES

INGREDIENTS

- glass bottles
- scissors
- tacky glue
- raffia

Add a dab of glue to end of raffia.

Press onto bottom of bottle and begin to wrap around and up.

Change colors, add a dab of glue, and wrap, wrap, wrap!

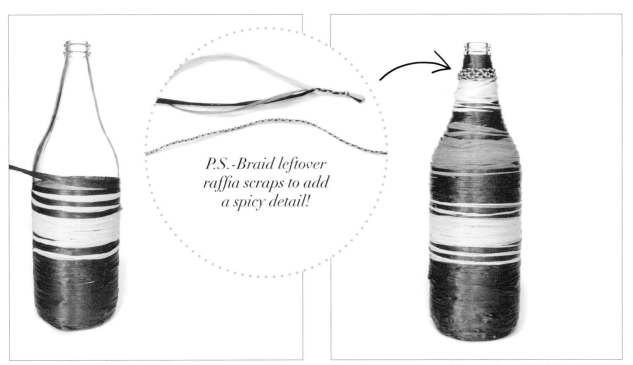

P.S.-Braid leftover raffia scraps to add a spicy detail!

Get creative and layer it up!

Continue to wrap until bottle is completely covered, then glue on braid.

P.S.-
KNOTTED
TASSEL
NECKLACE

INGREDIENTS

- chain
- nylon string
- scissors

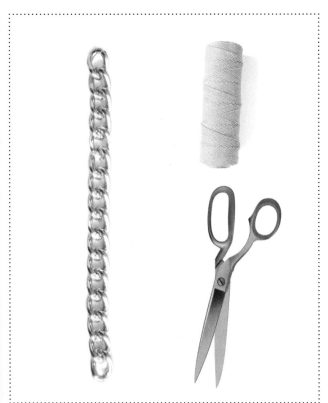

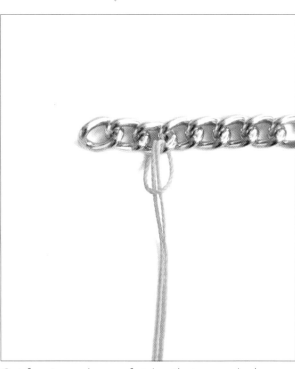

Cut fourteen pieces of string that are 17 inches long. Fold each in half, loop through center of chain link, then pull through and tighten.

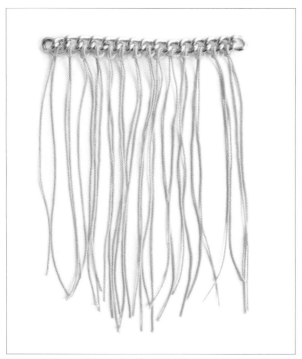

Loop strings through all chain links, leaving the two outside links open.

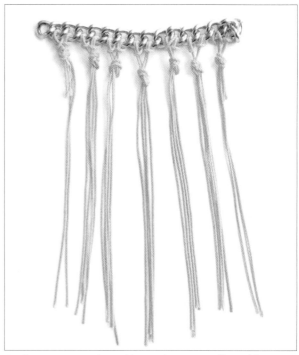

Gather two sections (four pieces total) and knot together, making sure knots line up at the top.

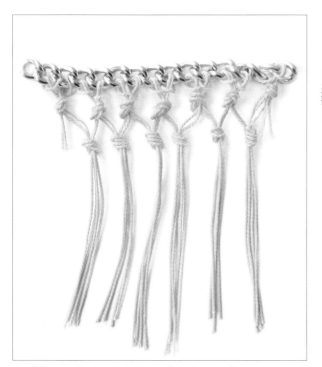

Gather two more sections, knot together in between the knots above . . . and continue.

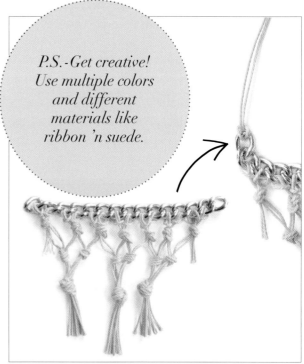

P.S.-Get creative! Use multiple colors and different materials like ribbon 'n suede.

Leave ends long, trimming to create even tassel ends. Loop and knot strings to finish.

FIESTA BARRETTE

BOBBY PINS

+

TWIST TIES

FAUX FLOWERS

RIBBON

do the craft math!

=

Look fly at your fiesta with a little flair in your hair. Use faux flowers from your local craft store to create an easy flowery accent with items you probably already have at home. Use twist ties to join flowers together, wrap ribbon to cover stems, and secure in hair with bobby pins for an accessory that's *delicioso*.

BE
smart

MAKE
DELICIOUS
ART

SEW SWEET!

Show your sweet side and butter up someone special by mixing creativity and smiles sprinkled with some feminine wiles. Combining flirty ingredients such as ladylike lace, regal pearls, flouncy organza, and dainty bows will step up your soirée faster than you can say sweet tooth. Setting the perfect tone and table always calls for whimsical flair. So whether you're drizzling a chandelier with sass or simply icing the cupcakes, delicate details will make all the difference and light up the room. Don't forget, a delicious DIY doesn't have to be edible; a lovely personal touch is just as scrumptious!

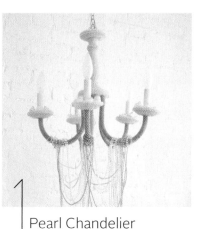

1 Pearl Chandelier

2 Lace Ballet Flat

3 Peplum Tee

4 Floral Bow Napkin Rings

P.S.-
PEARL CHANDELIER

INGREDIENTS

- chandelier
- white spray paint
- faux pearl beads 'n strands
- seashells
- glue gun

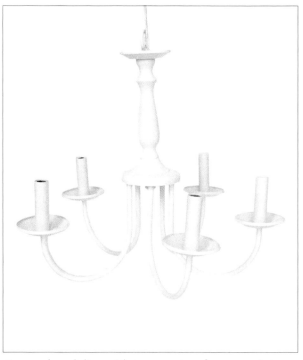

Cover chandelier with two coats of spray paint.

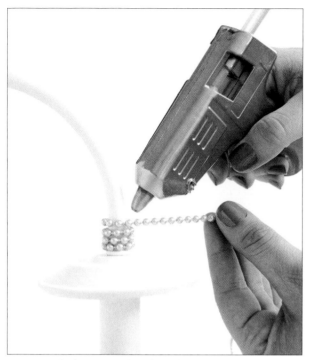

Wrap and glue strands of small plastic pearls around arms of chandelier.

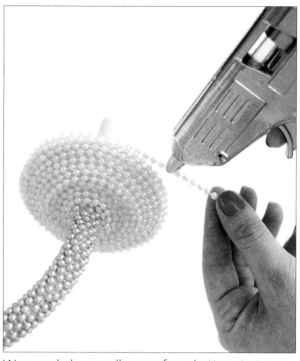

Wrap and glue candle cups from bottom to top.

Glue shells inside candle cups. (P.S.- add any other bits and bobs your heart desires!)

Drip, wrap, and continue to drape strands of pearls all over.

P.S.- ▶ this...
HOW-TO VIDEO

INGREDIENTS

- ballet flats
- scissors
- fabric glue
- lace trim

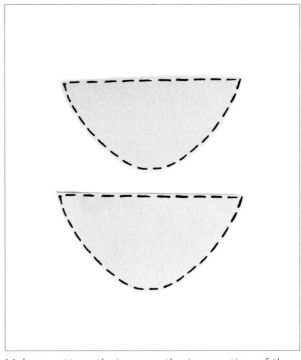

Make a pattern that covers the toe portion of the shoe, leaving an extra ½-inch border.

Trim lace to pattern and cut two narrow strips for the back of shoes.

Use glue to attach lace to front of shoe.

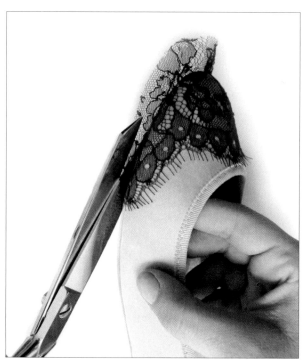

Wait until glue dries completely, then trim any excess lace.

Glue on back detail strip and allow to dry.

P.S.-
PEPLUM
TEE

INGREDIENTS

- tee shirt
- organza fabric
- Swiss Army knife
- straight pins
- needle 'n thread
- scissors

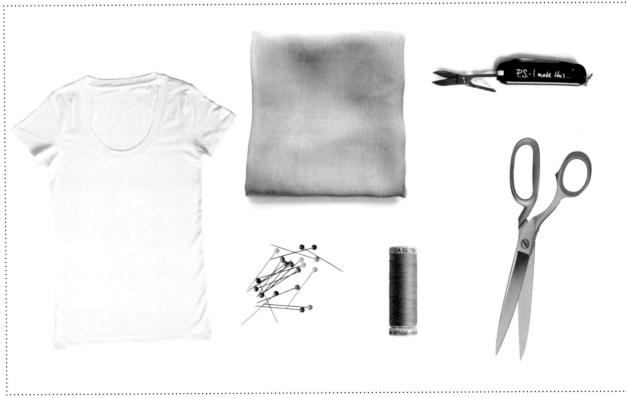

P.S.-I made this...

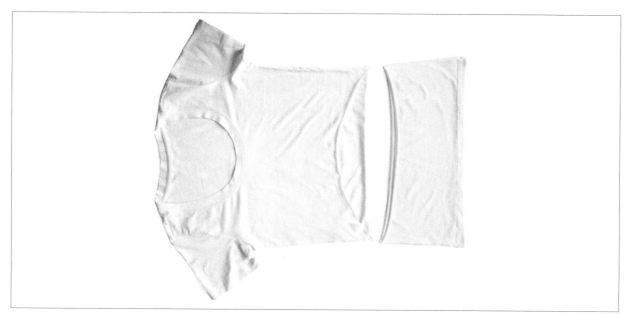

Cut off bottom third of shirt, then cut front hem in an arc.

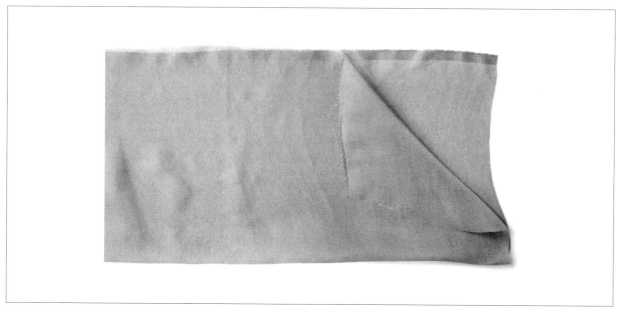

Cut an 18 x 64-inch piece of organza fabric and fold in half. (P.S.- size will vary according to your shirt.)

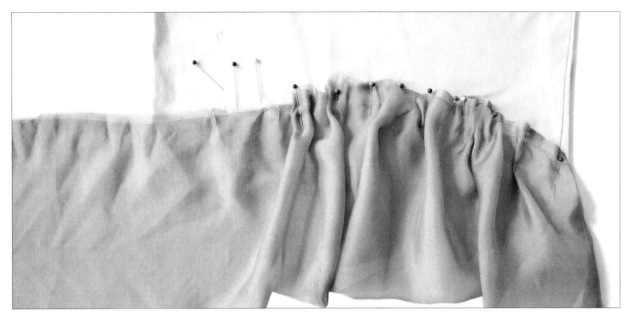

Gather and pin organza around bottom hem of shirt, overlapping 1 inch.

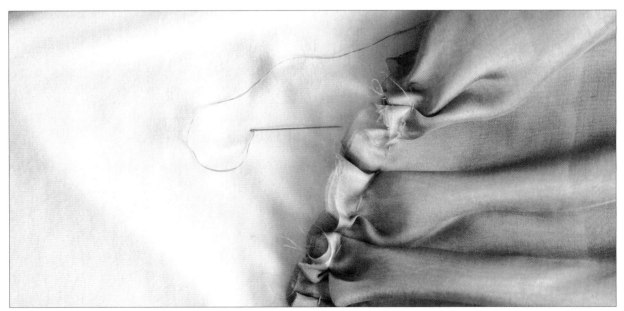

Sew organza onto shirt using a double-threaded needle.

Trim loose threads and any extra material for a clean edge.

*Put a
little extra
PEP
in your
STEP!*

P.S.-

FLORAL BOW
NAPKIN RINGS

INGREDIENTS

- patterned tee shirt or fabric
- fabric stiffener
- paintbrush
- cardboard paper towel tube
- scissors
- wax paper

P.S.-Lay wax paper under fabric before painting.

Cut tee shirt into 27 x 2-inch strips.

Paint an even coat of fabric stiffener directly onto fabric.

Tie and knot around paper towel roll when fabric is halfway stiffened.

Tie bow and let dry completely.

A day without
DIY
is like a day without
SUNSHINE

SPLENDID in the GRASS

There's no better way to spend a sun-drenched afternoon than by lounging with friends. The perfect picnic should be packed with equal parts delicious food and chic fashion. So spread your DIY wings (and a handcrafted blanket) while you take a moment to relax, smile, and enjoy the craftier things in life. After all, a day without DIY is like a day without sunshine! Whether you're planning a picnic or just thirsty to accessorize, you've come to the right place . . .

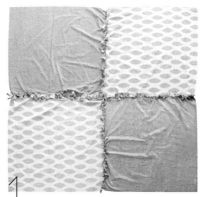

1 Patchwork Blanket

2 Faux-Stitch Fedora

3 Color Block Tote

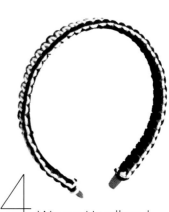

4 Woven Headband

P.S.-

PATCHWORK
BLANKET

INGREDIENTS

- 2 printed tablecloths or fabric

- measuring tape

- scissors

Cut fabric into four same-size squares, two of each pattern.

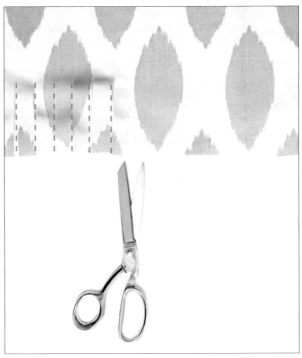

Cut 5-inch-long slits, 1 inch apart, along edges of fabric on two sides of each square.

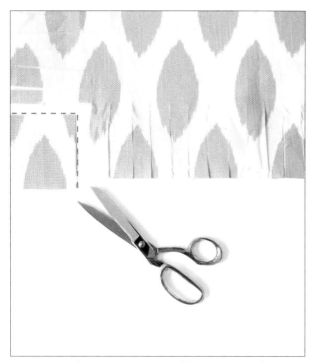

Cut a 5 x 5-inch square out of the corner where slits meet.

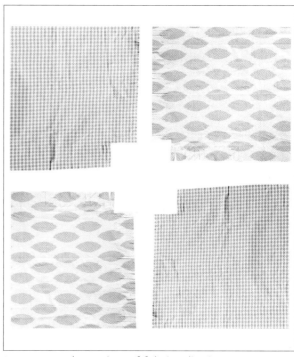

Lay out each section of fabric, aligning cutout corners to meet in the center.

Double knot the strips of cut fabric together.

P.S.- ▶ this...
HOW-TO VIDEO

P.S.- trim it if you fancy!

P.S.-

FAUX-STITCH
FEDORA

INGREDIENTS

- straw fedora hat

- colored silk ribbon

- two Sharpie markers

Plan out a pattern and "dot it" with two colored markers in contrasting colors.

Fill in each woven section by making small scribbles.

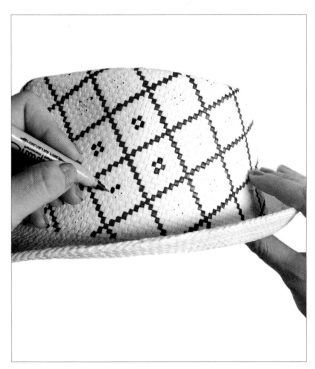

Fill in smaller details with the second color.

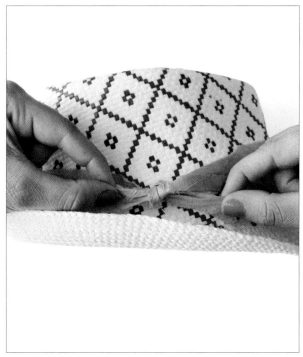

Tie and knot ribbon around the brim.

P.S.-

COLOR BLOCK TOTE

INGREDIENTS

- canvas tote bag
- paper tape
- acrylic paint
- pair of jeans
- foam paintbrush
- scissors
- glue gun

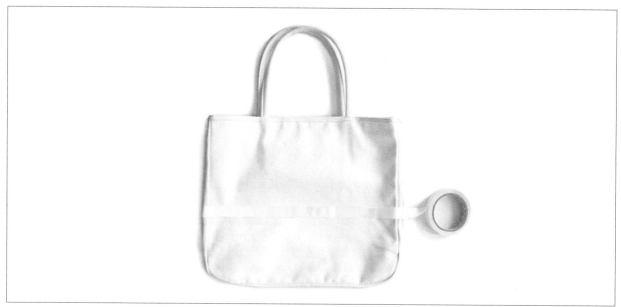

Block off the bottom section and top edge of tote with tape.

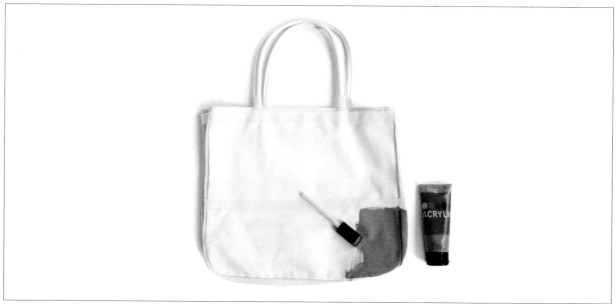

Paint a block of color around base and top edge.

Cut approximately 1½-inch-wide strips of denim from a pair of old jeans.

Listen to your denim...it's dying for a DIY!

Adhere strip with a dab of hot glue to one end of the handle and wrap the strip around to the other end, then glue again to seal.

Cut out back pockets of jeans.

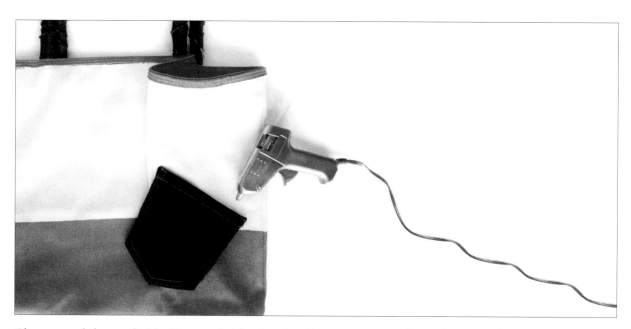

Glue around the pocket bottom and sides, leaving the top open, and attach one pocket to each end of tote.

P.S.-
WOVEN HEADBAND

INGREDIENTS

- headband
- scissors
- string
- suede lacing

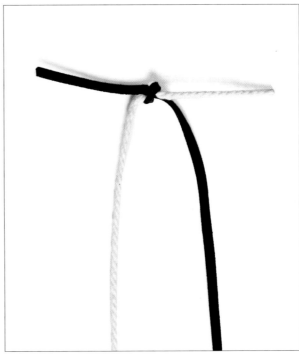

Cut 54 inches each of string and suede lacing and double knot them together. (P.S.- snip the ends.)

Secure with a double knot onto one end of headband and twist around to inside.

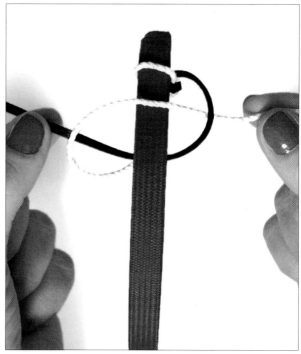

Cross one string over top and the other under the headband, creating an open knot, then pull top string through loop.

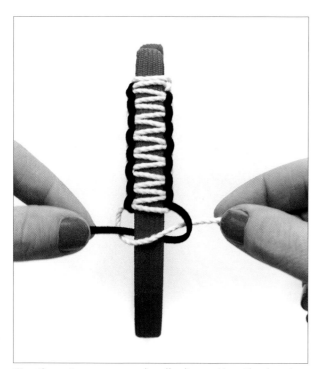

Continue to weave and pull, alternating the knots from side to side.

Tie a double knot when you reach the end and trim any excess string.

"*Crafternoon*" IS THE NEW GIRLS' NIGHT IN

GAME ON!

Luck be a lady who rolls the dice, so raise the stakes for your next cocktail party. Feeling like a high roller in the game of life is easy when you feel great and look phenomenal. Shuffle the decks, shake up some flirty cocktails, and bring your A-game style. As you ante up, remember to always keep it classy, from your accessories down to the smallest details. Double down on DIY to make your next girls' night in a real game changer!

1 Coin Charm Bracelet

2 Cork Clutch

3 Key Covers

4 Dahlia Cocktail Ring

P.S.-

COIN CHARM
BRACELET

INGREDIENTS

- Key identifiers
- jump rings
- toggle clasp

- coins
- chain
- pliers

Open jump ring and attach to key identifier.

Cut chain to desired length, then attach key identifers.

Attach toggle clasp to both ends.

Insert coins for a charming final touch.

P.S.-
CORK
CLUTCH

INGREDIENTS

- plastic pencil box
- cork paper
- Swiss Army Knife
- studs
- wine cork
- glitter blast spray
- heavy-duty glue
- foam paintbrush
- scissors

Apply a generous coat or two of glitter spray onto pencil case and wine cork.

Cut cork paper to fit on top of case (make slightly smaller to create border) and a strip that will be wrapped around wine cork.

Push and secure stud details into each corner of the cork paper.

slice it

glue it

stud it

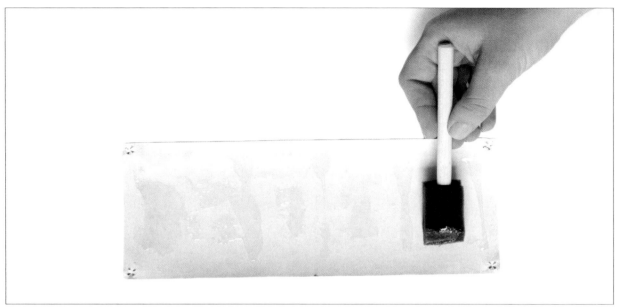

Spread an even layer of glue onto cork paper and adhere to case.

Use glue to attach faux toggle and hold in place until dry.

P.S.-
KEY COVERS

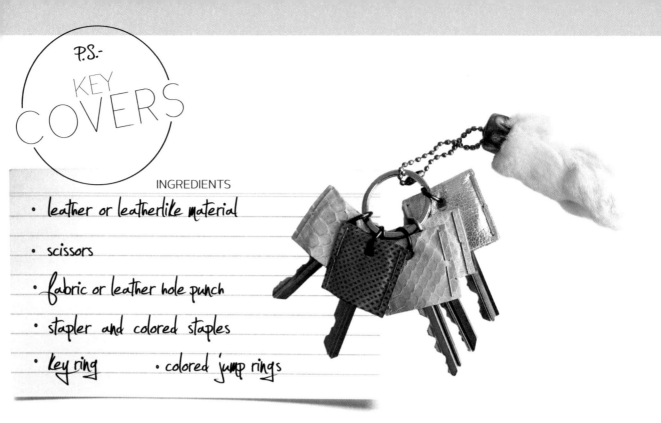

INGREDIENTS

- leather or leatherlike material
- scissors
- fabric or leather hole punch
- stapler and colored staples
- key ring   • colored jump rings

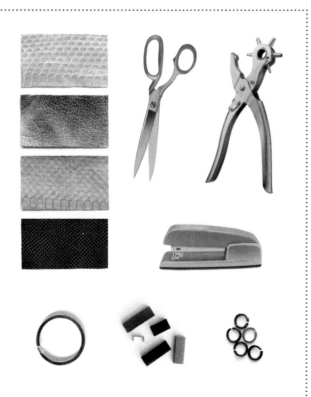

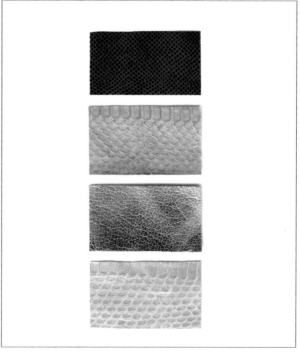

Cut material into 2½ x 1½-inch rectangles.

Fold rectangles in half and staple twice on two sides.

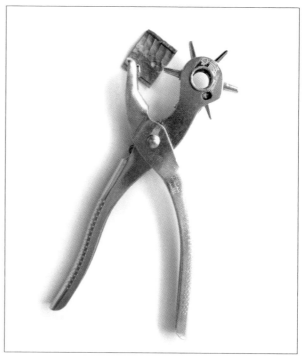

Create a hole at the top of each, using hole punch.

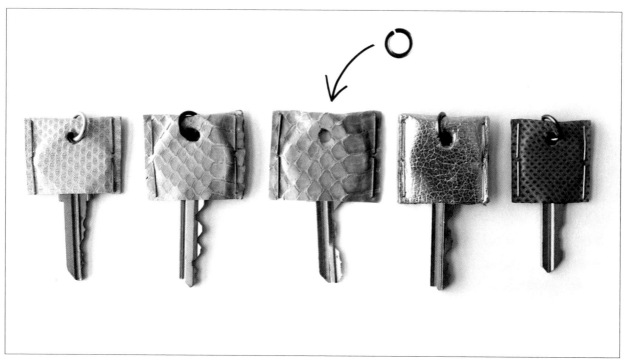

Slide key in cover and connect the two with a jump ring. Finish off by attaching them to a key ring.

P.S.-
DAHLIA COCKTAIL RING

INGREDIENTS

- outdoor faucet handle
- nail polish
- pearl bead
- 2 gauges of jewelry wire: thin 'n thick
- wire cutters

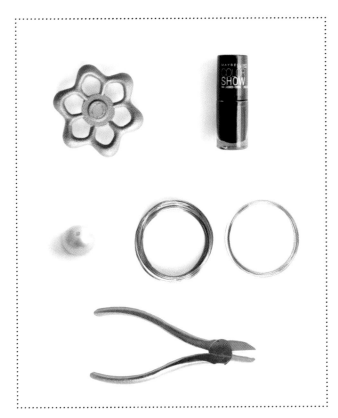

Paint valve handle with nail polish. You may need two coats, depending on the color.

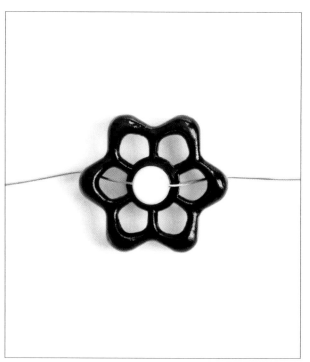

Thread wire through valve, add pearl bead, and pull wire through opposite side.

Wrap wire to secure pearl in place.

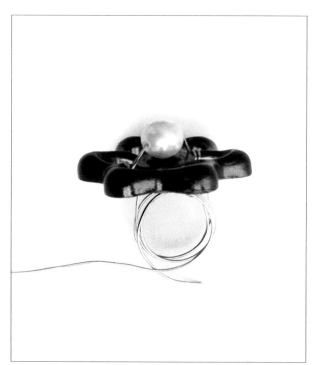

Measure the desired ring size and wrap wire accordingly.

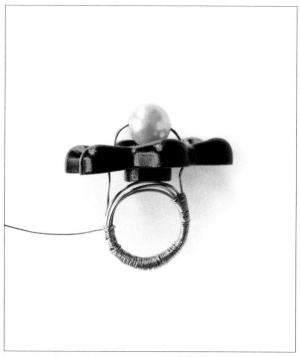

Use thin jewerly wire to wrap tightly around base of ring to finish.

GLITTER COASTERS

+

CARDBOARD
SQUARES

GLITTER
BLAST
SPRAY

do the craft math!

=

There's no rest for the weary, but there is one for your drinking glass . . . and it should be doused in glitter, of course! Impress your guests with a coaster made of cardboard squares and a few coats of Glitter Blast spray.

P.S.- (▶) this...
HOW-TO VIDEO

DIVE
into DIY

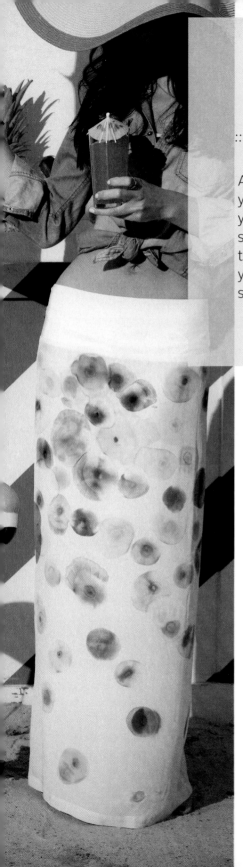

MAKE A SPLASH!

As the weather heats up, so should your style. Transform your beach club into a craft club by looking stellar when you soak up the sun with friends, and flood a summery setting with hot hues and cool accents. Unique touches that float from delicate skirts to side tables will anchor your style and set you apart from the rest. Don't skim the surface: take a deep dive into DIY for the perfect 10!

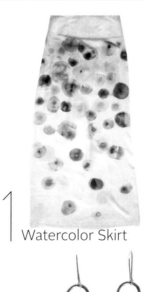

1 Watercolor Skirt

2 Turban Headband

3 Clear Cascade Earrings

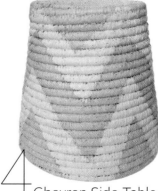

4 Chevron Side Table

P.S.-
WATERCOLOR SKIRT

INGREDIENTS

- silk skirt
- Sharpie markers
- rubber bands
- plastic cups
- rubbing alcohol
- eyedropper

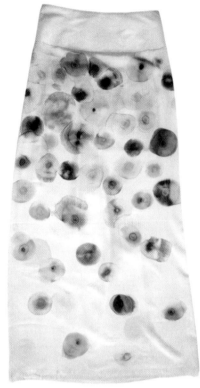

Stretch section of skirt over plastic cups and secure tightly with rubber bands.

Outline and fill in a circle using a bright-colored permanent marker.

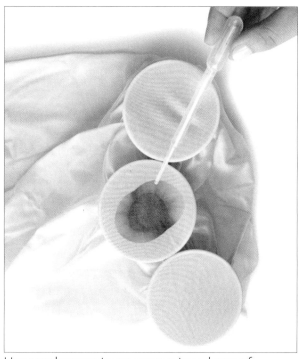

Use eyedropper to squeeze 3 to 5 drops of rubbing alcohol directly onto color.

Get creative and layer multiple colors.

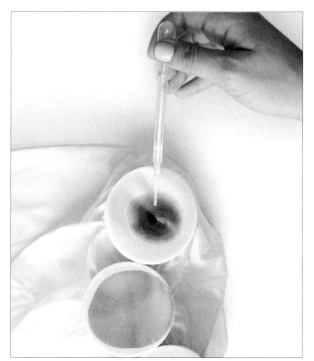

Repeat the cup and eyedropper process. P.S.- the more drops, the wider the color will bleed.

P.S.-
TURBAN HEADBAND

INGREDIENTS

- headband
- scissors
- raw silk fabric
- glue gun

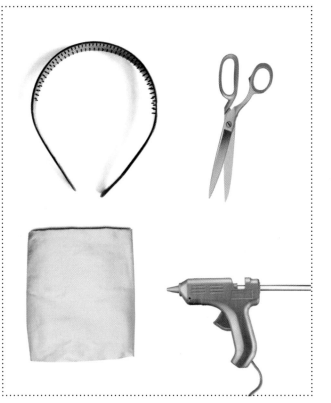

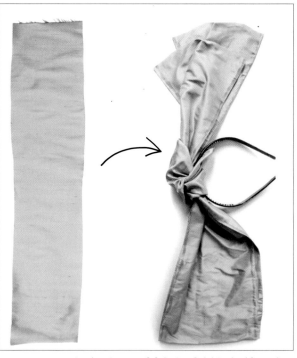

Cut a 36 x 6-inch piece of fabric, fold in half, and knot around top of headband.

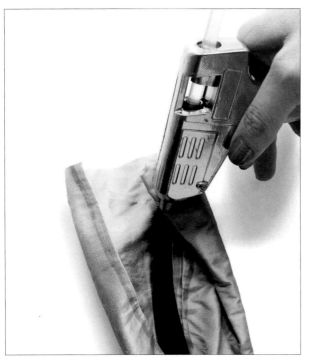

Fold one corner in and glue to base of headband.

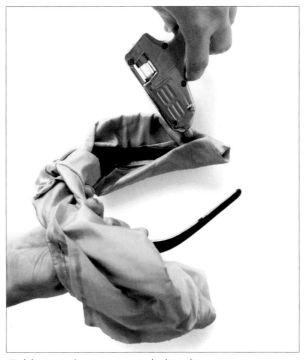

Fold opposite corner and glue down.

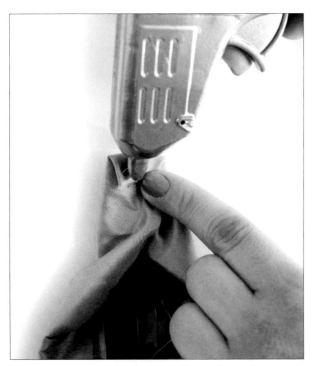

Fold bottom edge in and glue down for a clean end.

Take a bite out of this *WATERMELON POP video!*

P.S.- ▶ this...
HOW-TO VIDEO

P.S.-

CLEAR
CASCADE
EARRINGS

INGREDIENTS

- earring wires
- jump rings
- clear plastic tubing
- scissors
- pliers

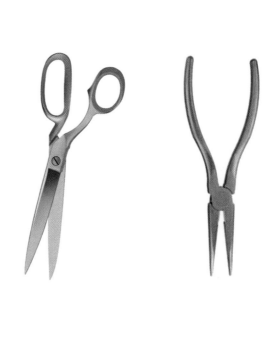

Cut tubing into thin rings.

Link and attach with jump rings.

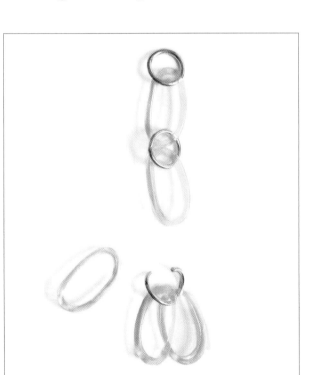

Combine three rings for bottom detail onto last jump ring.

Attach earring wire at the top.

P.S.-

CHEVRON
SIDE TABLE

INGREDIENTS

- straw basket
- newspaper
- paper tape
- 2 quarts acrylic house paint
- paintbrushes: thin 'n thick

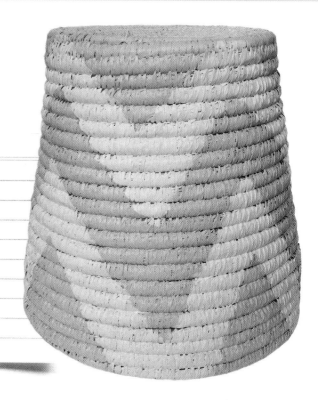

Cover and tape basket with newspaper, leaving the top exposed in an inverted triangle pattern, and paint.

After paint dries, cover and tape another section that follows the same lines as the top triangle pattern.

Paint a contrasting color that pops.

Use a small paintbrush to touch up details.

Top off the table with one last coat.

GOLD DOT SHADES

SUNGLASSES

GOLD
PUFFY
PAINT

do the craft math!

=

L ook no more: you've come to the right place for an eye-popping DIY. Add a chic Midas touch with a dot-infused quilted pattern on sunglasses with a little help from your friend "puffy paint."

BEFORE YOU KICK UP YOUR HEELS, EMBELLISH THEM!

CHEERS!

Create an evening to remember by following the rules of Party 101: wrangle your nearest and dearest and infuse a personal DIY touch from head to toe and ceiling to floor, then pop the cork and kick up your heels! Adhere to these simple rules and your fête will sparkle and shine into the early-morning hours. And make note: savvy and unique style is always required at the door. P.S.- bring it!

1 | Striped Champagne Flutes

2 | Feather Ankle Wrap

3 | Glam Wire Earrings

4 | Crystal Barrel Necklace

P.S.-

STRIPED CHAMPAGNE FLUTES

INGREDIENTS

- champagne flutes

- assorted nail polish

- clear nail polish

Paint a stripe of nail polish around the top of the flute's stem.

Paint another . . .

And another . . .

Seal the deal with a coat of clear!

And another . . .

Make a toast to the host . . . and P.S.- hand wash only!

P.S.-

FEATHER
ANKLE WRAP

INGREDIENTS

- black velvet ribbon

- peacock feather trim

- fabric glue

- Velcro

- scissors

Measure ribbon and feather trim to fit the circumference of your ankle; leave an extra inch on the end of ribbon.

Align the top of feather trim to the middle of ribbon and attach with glue.

Fold the top half of ribbon over feather trim. Press firmly and wait until dry.

Once glue is dry, place a 1-inch strip of Velcro on inside and outside where ends overlap.

GLAM WIRE
EARRINGS

INGREDIENTS

- paper clips

- safety pins in various sizes

- thin jewelry wire

- earring wires

- wire cutters

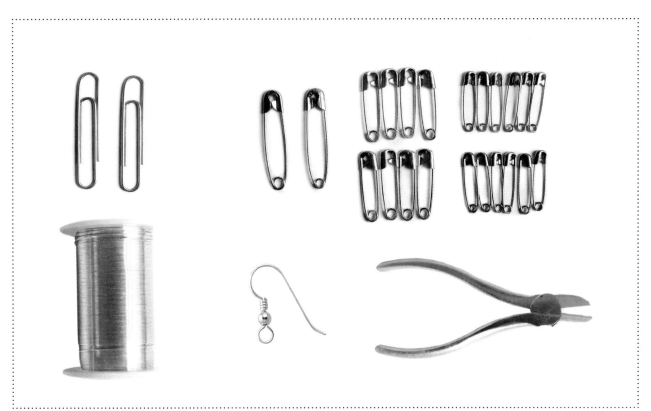

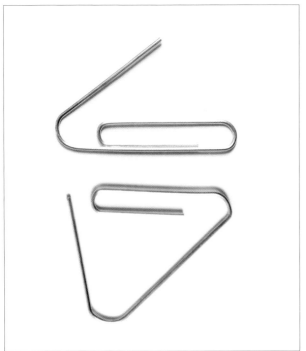

Unfold paper clips into two triangles.

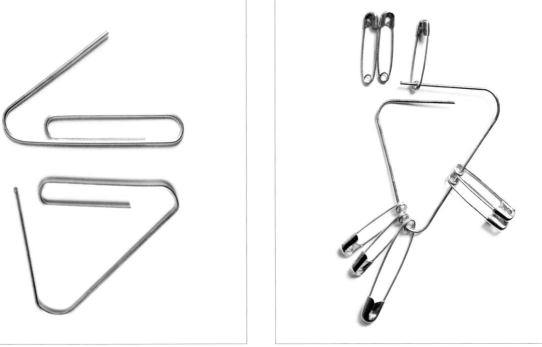

Slip on safety pins, creating a cascade with smaller pins on the sides and larger in the middle.

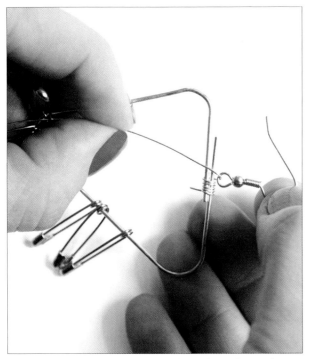

Wrap thin jewelry wire around both ends to close triangle, slipping earring wire in the center.

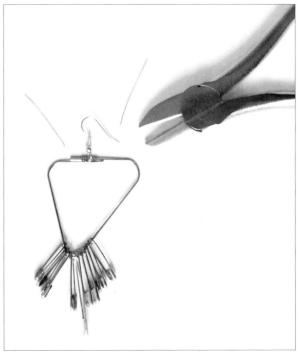

Snip ends of wire.

CRYSTAL
BARREL
NECKLACE

INGREDIENTS

- 1 yard ribbon
- Swarovski crystal cupchain
- climbing rope
- scissors
- glue gun

Cut an 18-inch length of rope.

Have a FLING with BLING!

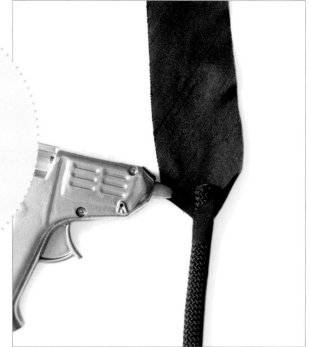

Cut ribbon in half, and glue one piece of ribbon to each end of rope.

Knot ribbon at ends to cover rope.

Wrap and glue crystal cupchain from end to end.

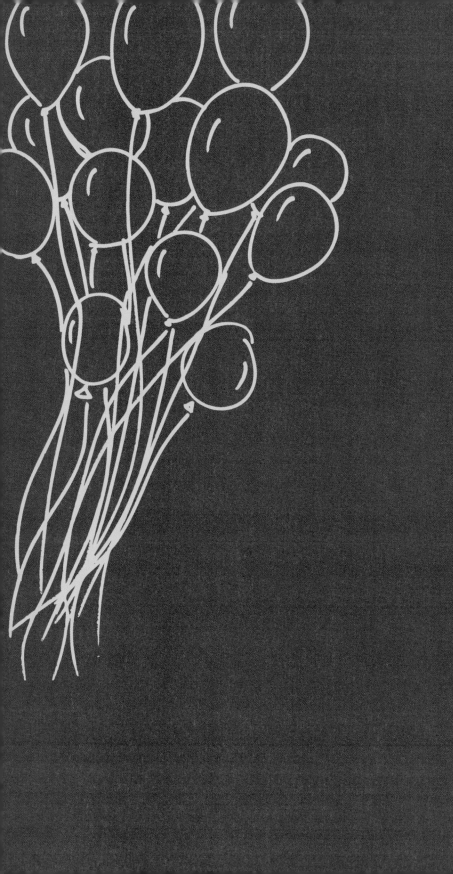

Celebrate
WHAT'S IN YOUR
HEART

GO BRIGHT
or GO HOME

When life gives you lemons, make delicious pink lemonade and a bold necklace, and throw a punchy party! It's a known fact that the brighter the color, the bigger the smile, so paint your celebration into a portrait of radiant memories by adding bold, fun, and creative touches. Adding extra doses of peppy colors in unexpected places from bookshelves to tabletops will make your guests ooh and ahh over and over. Don't be afraid to infuse spunky eye-catching colors into your DIYs and everyday style. There's a vibrant hue overhaul with your name on it . . . get involved!

1 Bookshelf Inserts

2 Heart Bib Necklace

3 Neon Tube Bracelets

4 Rope Message Art

P.S.-
BOOKSHELF
INSERTS

INGREDIENTS

- cardboard
- duct tape
- ruler
- wrapping paper
- scissors

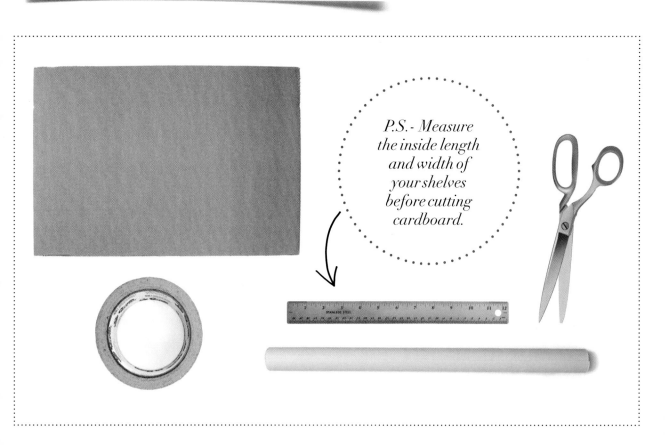

P.S.- Measure the inside length and width of your shelves before cutting cardboard.

Roll out wrapping paper on a flat surface, placing cardboard insert on top, and cut.

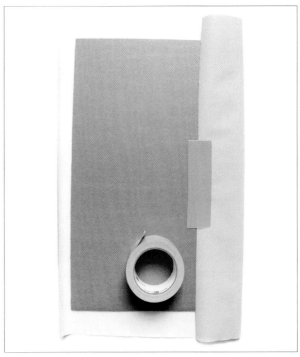

Use tape to secure one side of paper to cardboard.

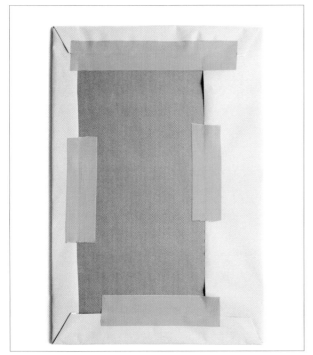

Continue to fold and tape each side.

Be sure to wrap each insert tightly for a clean and chic look.

P.S.-

HEART BIB
NECKLACE

INGREDIENTS

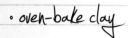

- oven-bake clay
- baking sheet
- ribbon
- mini heart-shaped cookie cutter
- jump rings
- rolling pin
- cocktail straw

Flatten clay into one ¼-inch-thick piece using rolling pin.

Use cookie cutter to cut hearts from clay.

Use a cocktail straw to create holes, being sure to line up the hearts so jump rings connect properly.

ROLL IT.
CUT IT.
BAKE IT.
HEART IT!

♥

Bake clay at heat and time suggested. Once cooled, connect with jump rings.

Finish by double knotting desired length of ribbon onto each end.

P.S.-
ROPE MESSAGE ART

INGREDIENTS

- ornate frame
- matte spray paint
- measuring tape
- foamcore
- utility knife
- Sharpie marker
- glue
- neon rope
- paper tape

Spray frame with two coats of spray paint.

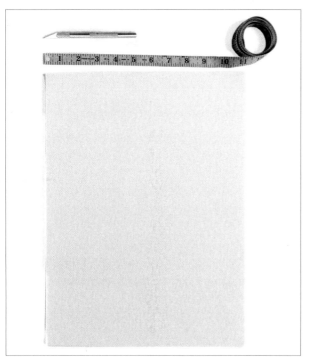

Measure and cut foamcore to fit back of frame.

Write a lovely message, then trace handwriting with glue.

Place rope onto glue, pressing into place.

Tape foamcore onto back of frame.

NEON TUBE
BRACELETS

INGREDIENTS

- latex tubing
- scissors
- hex nuts
- washers

P.S.- Take a trip to your local tackle shop to find this in a bevy of colors.

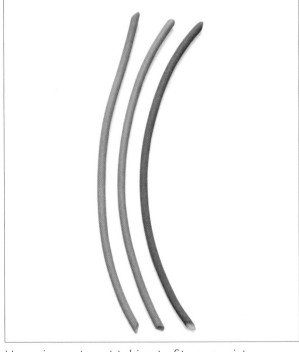

Use scissors to cut tubing to fit your wrist.

Slip washers and hex nuts onto tubing.

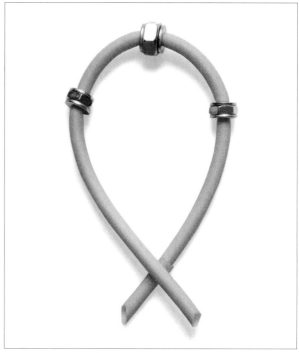

Get creative with patterns!

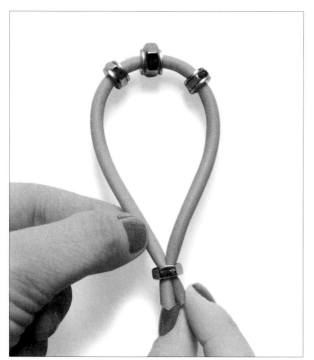

Slide a small hex nut onto both ends to finish.

Voilà!

DOTTED
TABLE EDGE

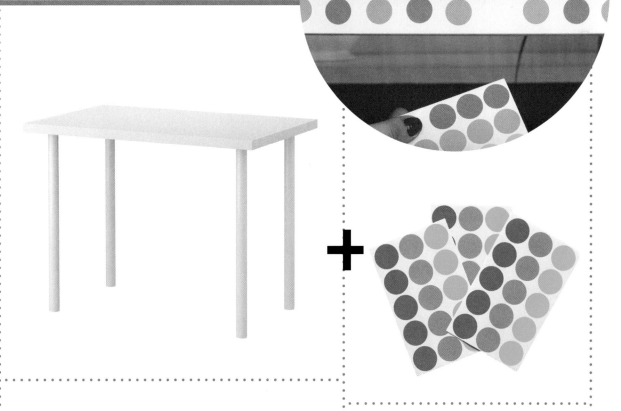

TABLE

+

DOT
LABELS

do the
craft math!

=

Have an inside edge on a stylish setting by adding a vibrant outside edge to a table. Stick bright dot labels around the edge for a fun dose of design that's quirky and super cute!

P.S.- ▶ this...
HOW-TO VIDEO

COOK UP *a* LITTLE *CREATIVITY*

SERVICE with a STYLE

Home is where the art is. Nothing tops a dinner party with your dearest friends and delicious food. Being the hostess with the mostess is easy after mastering the basic recipe for sophisticated style. Get inspired and cook up standout accessories from belts to bows . . . or opt for a tabletop touch that leaves guests gazing while guzzling over mercury glass candlestick holders. An infusion of DIY is easy to swallow and leaves the best aftertaste of all . . . compliments!

1 Mercury Glass Candlestick Holders

2 Lace Cap-Sleeve Shirt

3 Charm Belt

4 Elastic Shoe Bows

P.S.-

MERCURY GLASS
CANDLESTICK
HOLDERS

INGREDIENTS

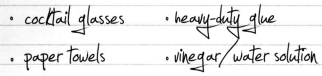

- cocktail glasses
- paper towels
- looking glass spray paint
- heavy-duty glue
- vinegar/water solution
- spray bottle

Coat the outside of each glass with spray paint.

Spray mixture of 1 part water, 1 part vinegar onto glass.

Dab and wipe using a paper towel to create a spotted and aged effect.

After it's completely dry, turn upside down and squeeze glue onto bottom of glass.

Add a second glass, hold in place, allow to set, and repeat with another glass.

P.S.- ▶ this...
HOW-TO VIDEO

P.S.-

CAP-SLEEVE
LACE
SHIRT

INGREDIENTS

- lace
- tank top
- needle 'n thread
- straight pins
- scissors

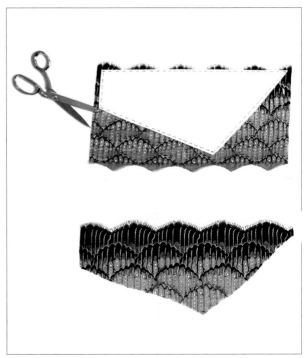

Make a pattern and cut out two lace pieces. (Size will vary according to person.)

Pin lace onto front side of neckline.

Continue to pin around the back; repeat with second lace piece on opposite shoulder.

Stitch onto shirt with a double-threaded needle.

Continue to stitch on the back.

P.S.-
CHARM
BELT

INGREDIENTS

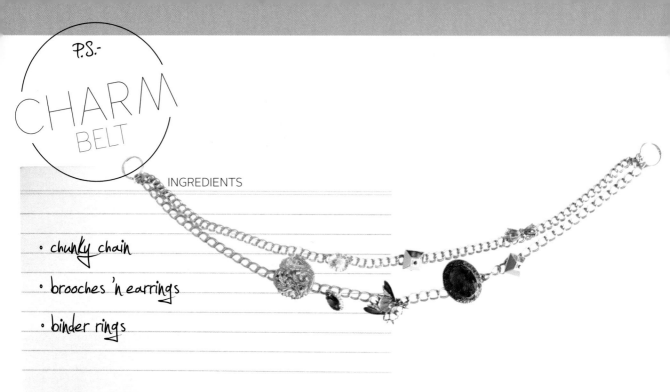

- chunky chain
- brooches 'n earrings
- binder rings

Rev up your DIY drive... make a convertible accessory!

Arrange jewelry along chain.

Clip and pin to secure in place.

P.S. - make sure all the backs are closed!

Attach binder rings to ends of chain to join.

P.S.-

ELASTIC
SHOE BOWS

INGREDIENTS

- leather or leatherlike material

- scissors

- pinking shears

- hair elastics

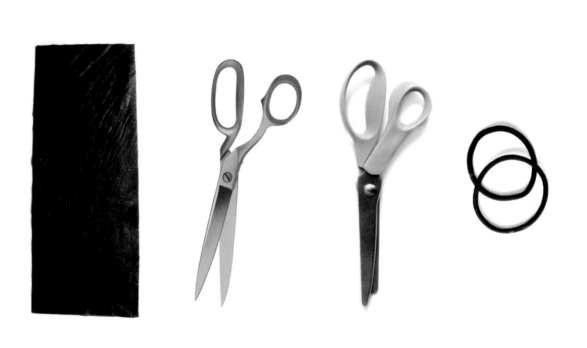

P.S.-Use pinking shears to trim edges of material for a fun zig-zag detail.

Use scissors to cut two 3½ x 2-inch rectangles and two ¼-inch-wide strips.

Lay long strip facedown, placing rectangle (pinched in the center and facedown) and hair elastic on top. Pull strip through elastic.

Knot once . . .

Knot twice . . . and snip.

If you want to take a ride on a *magic carpet...*

MAKE ONE!

DESTINATION DIY

Listen to your international inner muse because she's dying to whisk you away. With inspiration as your passport, it's easy to transport yourself to a magical setting without hopping on a plane. Create a regal staycation with euphoric style, where patterns and colors have no limits. Whether you need a style departure or an inventive BFF odyssey, designing a destination in your own backyard goes a long way!

1 Mirrored Pillow Covers

2 Jewel Printed Tank

3 Moroccan Tile Mirror

4 Tassel Hoop Earrings

P.S.-
MIRRORED
PILLOW
COVERS

INGREDIENTS

- pillow covers
- colored burlap
- craft mirror discs
- fabric glue
- heavy-duty glue

- needle 'n thread
- tassels
- scissors
- wax paper

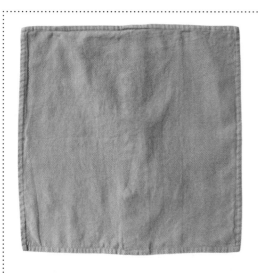

Glue mirror to burlap.

Cut out, leaving a ¼-inch border.

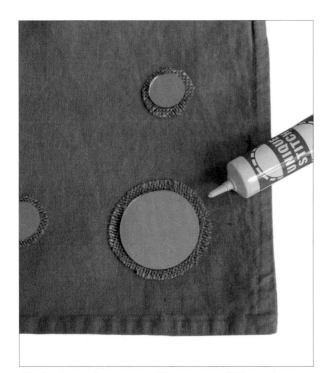

Glue mirror discs onto pillow cover. (Slip a piece of wax paper inside cover before you glue.)

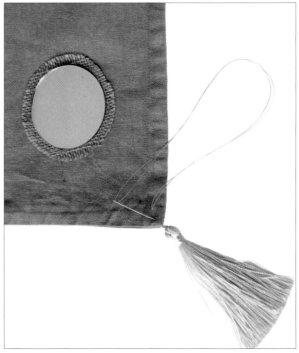

Sew and secure a tassel onto each corner of the pillow cover with a double-threaded needle.

INGREDIENTS

- tank top
- corks in various sizes
- cardboard
- fabric paint
- Swiss Army knife
- paintbrush

Paint bottom of largest cork.

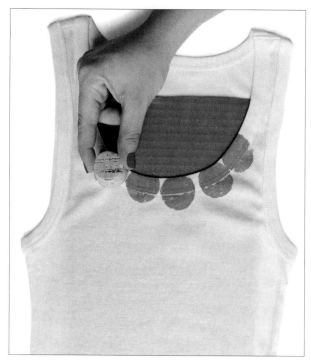

Slide cardboard inside shirt and press painted cork onto neckline—repaint cork bottom before each stamp—repeating pattern all the way around.

Paint a new color on a smaller cork and continue to create your pattern.

P.S.-Slice 'em into different shapes for a unique design.

Slice cork with knife to create half-moon shape to add to design.

Use small-bristle paintbrush to add final details.

P.S.-

MOROCCAN TILE
MIRROR

INGREDIENTS

- faux tin tile
- mirror
- foamcore
- Sharpie marker
- heavy-duty glue
- utility knife
- scissors

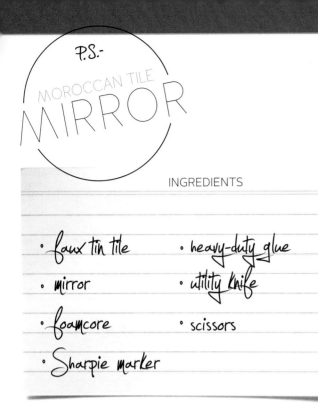

Draw large shape directly onto surface of tile.

118

P.S.-Use the utility knife or a box cutter to kick off the cutting process.

Cut out shape using sharp scissors.

Squeeze an ample amount of glue directly onto back of tile.

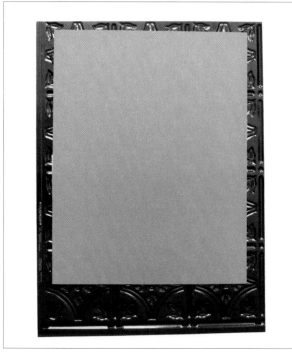

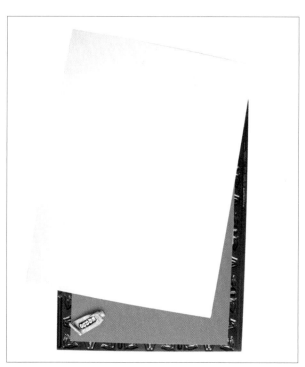

Place mirror, front side down, directly onto glue.

After glue dries, back mirror with heavy foamcore to support frame.

P.S.-
TASSEL HOOP
EARRINGS

INGREDIENTS

- earring hoops
- embroidery thread
- large 'n small metallic beads
- Swiss Army knife

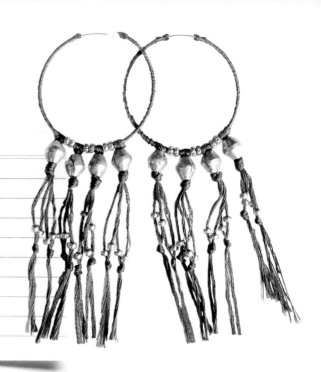

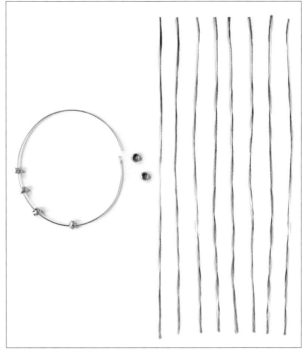

For each earring, slide six small beads onto earring hoop. Cut eight 8⅝-inch-long lengths of thread.

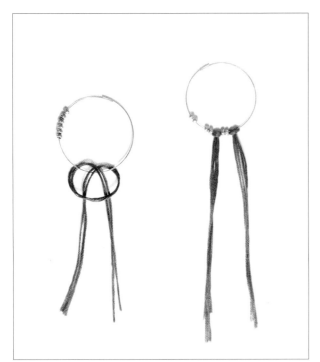

Take two pieces of thread, loop around and through the hoop, and pull tight to create a four-strand tassel, two beads apart.

Slide larger beads onto each tassel, knotting underneath each one to hold in place.

Knot and wrap thread around hoop. Add tiny beads to single strands of tassel. Knot two strands of tassel below single beads.

Snip ends of thread to make bottom of tassels even.

DIP-DYE RUGS

+

RUG

FABRIC DYE

do the craft math!

=

Fall in love over and over again with an overdyed rug. Repurpose an ornate rug that's begging for an update. Infuse with a rich color of fabric dye or get creative and mix your own hue!

P.S.- ▶ this...
HOW-TO VIDEO

TURN YOUR *DREAMS* INTO **DIY**s

S'MORE GIRL TIME

Roughing it never looked so good! Take an al fresco approach to girl time with Mother Nature as your partner in crime. Fashion and the great outdoors are strong advocates for risk taking and cultivating beauty, and it's easy to stand out in your neck of the woods when you're draped in a cape or looking fantastic with fringe. Pack essential ingredients for s'mores and killer DIY projects, and cozy up to a campfire near you for an eco-chic outing!

1 Aztec Print Poncho

2 Bootie Covers

3 Gilded Vases

4 Woven Clutch

P.S.-

AZTEC PRINT
PONCHO

INGREDIENTS

- printed fleece blanket

- scissors

Fold blanket in half horizontally.

P.S.-Be sure to cut through only the top layer!

Find center point and cut out a panel with a triangular top that will serve as the neckline.

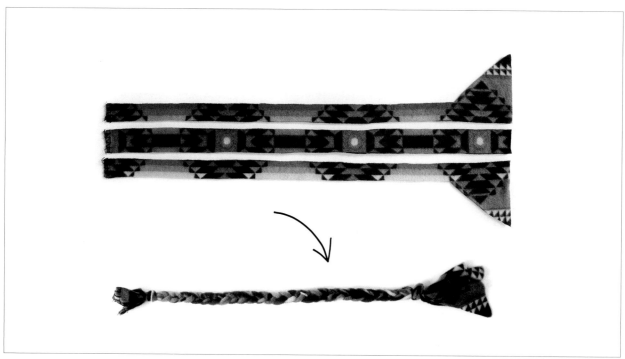

Cut panel into three pieces. Knot one end and braid to make a belt. Knot other end and stretch.

Make a 1-inch slit on each side, at waistline, 14 inches from front opening, for belt holes.

Drape fabric around body, weave belt through holes . . . tie, and look fab!

INGREDIENTS

- booties
- felt
- Velcro
- straight pins
- scissors
- fabric glue
- needle 'n thread
- 2 buttons

Cut felt into two 18¾ x 9-inch rectangles.

P.S. - You don't always need to keep your bootie covered... slip it on 'n off as you wish!

Fold long sides in and pin. Fold one end on a slight diagonal and pin.

Glue underside edges down with glue and let dry completely.

Match up inside and outside edges where bootie cover will close, and attach Velcro.

Sew button detail on outside and slip onto bootie.

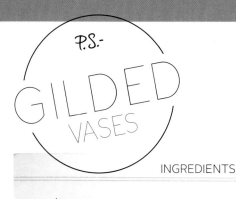

P.S.-

GILDED
VASES

INGREDIENTS

- glass vases
- gold metallic spray paint
- gold star stickers
- paper tape

*P.S.-Earn
your gold star
by sticking
a bunch on
a vase!*

Use tape to create varying graphic and bold patterns.

Cover each vase with two coats of spray paint.

After paint dries completely, carefully peel off tape.

P.S.- a slow pull is a clean pull . . . take your time!

P.S.-

WOVEN CLUTCH

INGREDIENTS

- leather or leatherlike material
- canvas pouch
- felt
- bangle (optional)
- ruler
- Sharpie marker
- scissors
- fabric or leather glue

136

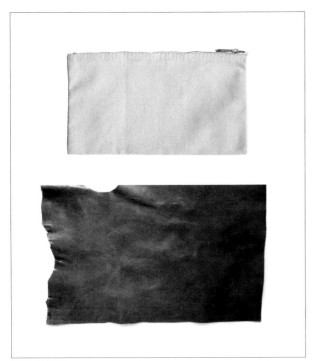

Cut two pieces of leather, one to overhang the width, and double the length of pouch for fringe, and a second for weaving horizontal strips.

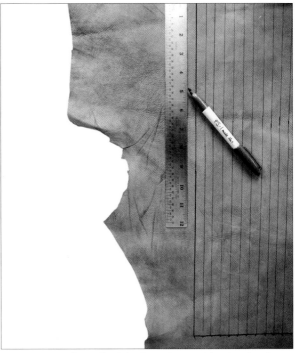

Measure and mark ½-inch strips on the back of both pieces.

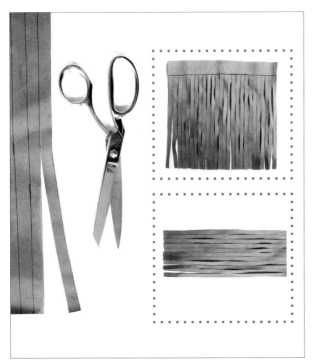

Piece 1: Create fringe (leaving a 2-inch top border).
Piece 2: Cut loose strips for weaving.

Weave loose strips over and under horizontally.

Pull pieces gently from all sides to create a tight basket-weave effect.

Glue a piece of felt to back.

Attach woven piece to front of pouch with glue.

Cut strips to create thin fringe at bottom of bag.

Trim ends to make even.

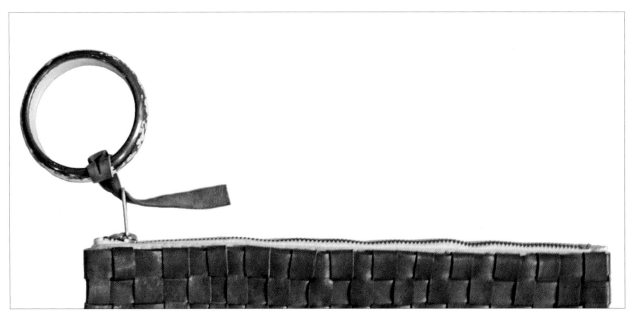

P.S.- for extra pizzazz, wrangle some wrist candy (a.k.a. a bangle) for a final touch!

GOLDEN TREE STUMP SIDE TABLE

+

TREE
STUMP

GOLD
SPRAY
PAINT

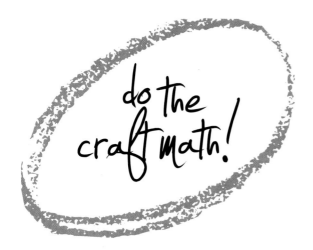

do the craft math!

$$=$$

Having metallic accents in your life will make you shine even brighter. Find a friend in Mother Nature simultaneously as you find and repurpose a tree stump for a perfect side table. With two or three heavy coats of gold spray paint and proper drying time, you're in business.

P.S.- ▶ *this...*
HOW-TO VIDEO

I SEE I
I LIKE I
I MAKI

*Turn your inspiration into reality...
Dive into this essential guide for all
of your **DIY** shopping needs!*

T. IT. E IT.
IT. E IT.

Don't wait for a get-together to GET IT TOGETHER!

...and here's where to buy it

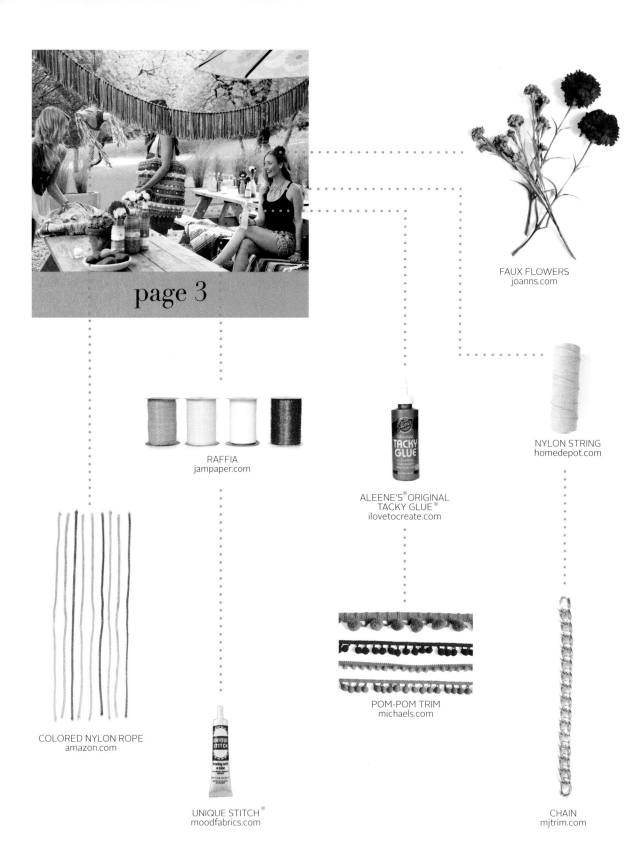

page 3

FAUX FLOWERS
joanns.com

RAFFIA
jampaper.com

ALEENE'S® ORIGINAL
TACKY GLUE®
ilovetocreate.com

NYLON STRING
homedepot.com

COLORED NYLON ROPE
amazon.com

POM-POM TRIM
michaels.com

UNIQUE STITCH®
moodfabrics.com

CHAIN
mjtrim.com

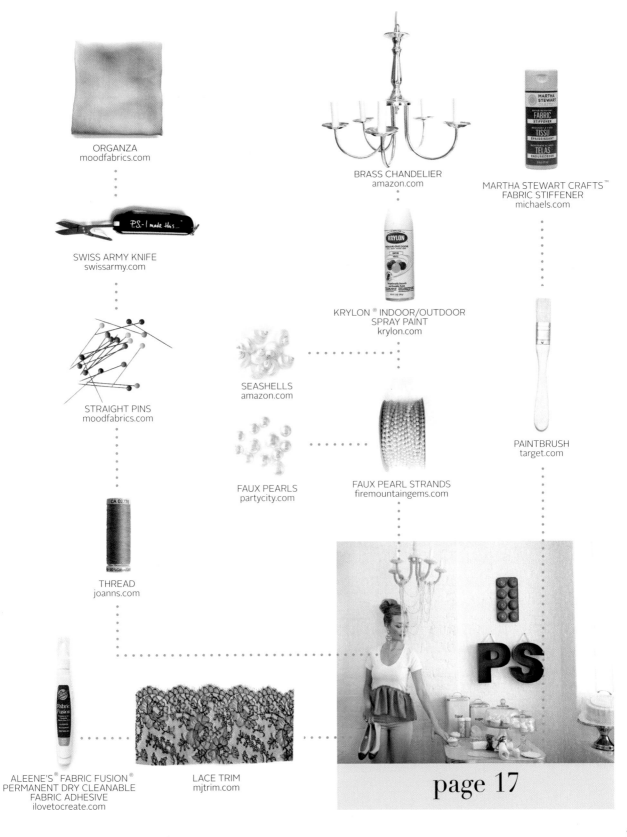

ORGANZA
moodfabrics.com

SWISS ARMY KNIFE
swissarmy.com

STRAIGHT PINS
moodfabrics.com

THREAD
joanns.com

ALEENE'S® FABRIC FUSION®
PERMANENT DRY CLEANABLE
FABRIC ADHESIVE
ilovetocreate.com

LACE TRIM
mjtrim.com

BRASS CHANDELIER
amazon.com

MARTHA STEWART CRAFTS™
FABRIC STIFFENER
michaels.com

KRYLON® INDOOR/OUTDOOR
SPRAY PAINT
krylon.com

SEASHELLS
amazon.com

FAUX PEARLS
partycity.com

FAUX PEARL STRANDS
firemountaingems.com

PAINTBRUSH
target.com

page 17

145

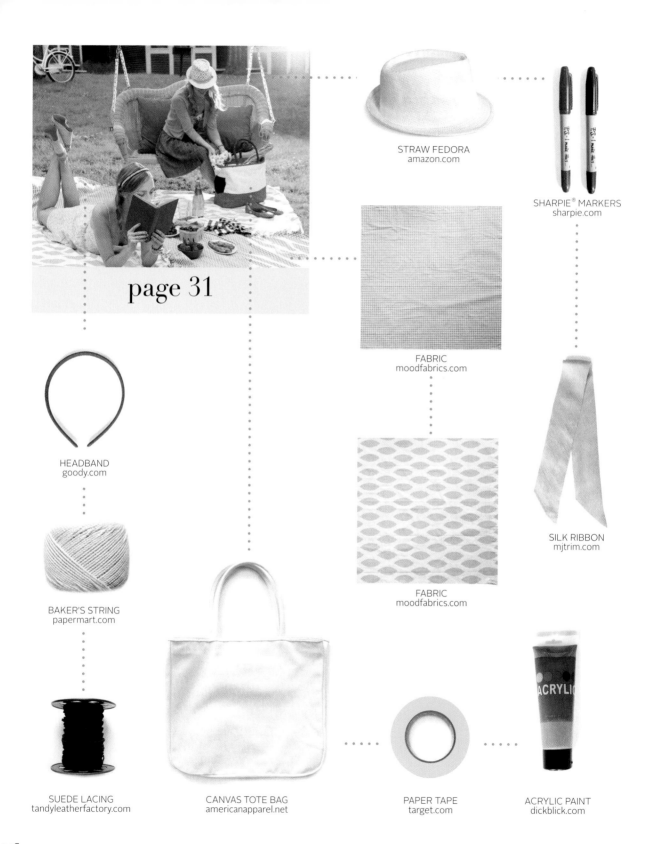

STRAW FEDORA
amazon.com

SHARPIE® MARKERS
sharpie.com

page 31

FABRIC
moodfabrics.com

HEADBAND
goody.com

SILK RIBBON
mjtrim.com

BAKER'S STRING
papermart.com

FABRIC
moodfabrics.com

SUEDE LACING
tandyleatherfactory.com

CANVAS TOTE BAG
americanapparel.net

PAPER TAPE
target.com

ACRYLIC PAINT
dickblick.com

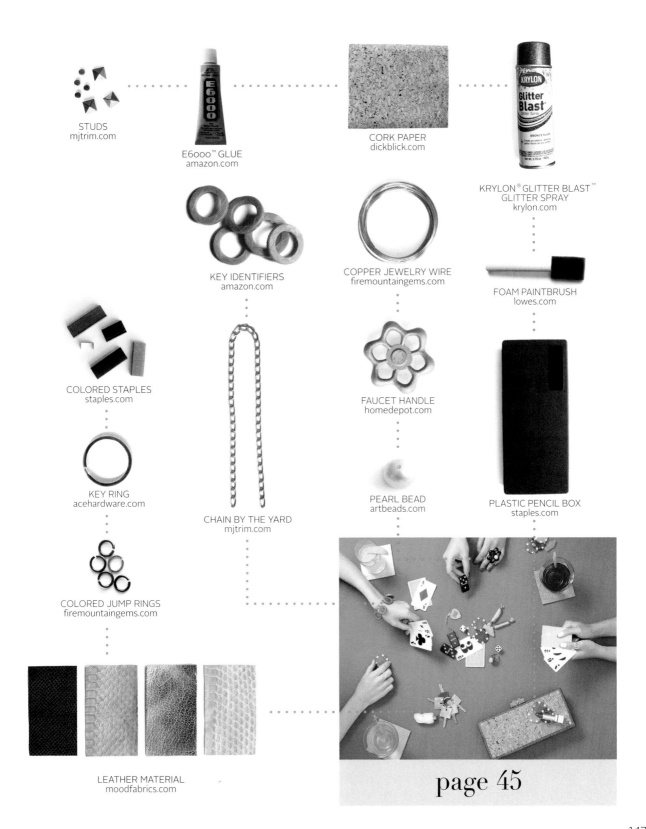

STUDS
mjtrim.com

E6000™ GLUE
amazon.com

CORK PAPER
dickblick.com

KRYLON® GLITTER BLAST™
GLITTER SPRAY
krylon.com

KEY IDENTIFIERS
amazon.com

COPPER JEWELRY WIRE
firemountaingems.com

FOAM PAINTBRUSH
lowes.com

COLORED STAPLES
staples.com

FAUCET HANDLE
homedepot.com

KEY RING
acehardware.com

CHAIN BY THE YARD
mjtrim.com

PEARL BEAD
artbeads.com

PLASTIC PENCIL BOX
staples.com

COLORED JUMP RINGS
firemountaingems.com

LEATHER MATERIAL
moodfabrics.com

page 45

PAINT
lowes.com

RAW SILK FABRIC
moodfabrics.com

PAINTBRUSH
hobbylobby.com

PLASTIC TUBING
homedepot.com

TULIP® 3D FABRIC PAINT
ilovetocreate.com

EARRING WIRES
michaels.com

STRAW BASKET
containerstore.com

HEADBAND
goody.com

JUMP RINGS
michaels.com

page 61

SHARPIE® MARKERS
sharpie.com

EYEDROPPER
amazon.com

RUBBER BANDS
staples.com

NAIL POLISH
maybelline.com

GOLD SAFETY PINS
kmart.com

CLIMBING ROPE
ems.com

JEWELRY WIRE
firemountaingems.com

SWAROVSKI CRYSTAL
CUPCHAIN
jewelrysupply.com

VELVET RIBBON
joann.com

CHAMPAGNE FLUTES
cb2.com

EARRING WIRES
firemountaingems.com

FEATHER TRIM
mjtrim.com

page 75

149

page 87

LATEX TUBING
westmarine.com

HEX NUTS
homedepot.com

ORNATE FRAME
ebay.com

WASHERS
homedepot.com

SCULPEY III®
OVEN-BAKE CLAY
acmoore.com

ELMER'S® GLUE-ALL®
officedepot.com

DUCT TAPE
duckbrand.com

MINI COOKIE CUTTER
wilton.com

KRYLON® INDOOR/OUTDOOR
SPRAY PAINT
krylon.com

NEON ROPE
homedepot.com

WRAPPING PAPER
target.com

BINDER RINGS
staples.com

BROOCHES & EARRINGS
ebay.com

LEATHER MATERIAL
moodfabrics.com

PINKING SHEARS
michaels.com

COCKTAIL GLASSES
target.com

SPRAY BOTTLE
target.com

KRYLON® LOOKING GLASS™
SPRAY PAINT
krylon.com

TANK TOP
forever21.com

LACE
mjtrim.com

page 101

page 113

EARRING HOOPS
firemountaingems.com

METALLIC BEADS
firemountaingems.com

EMBROIDERY THREAD
joann.com

FAUX TIN TILE
homedepot.com

MIRROR
target.com

CORKS
createforless.com

BURLAP
moodfabrics.com

MIRROR DISCS
mjtrim.com

FABRIC PAINT
ilovetocreate.com

RUG
bedbathandbeyond.com

RIT ® DYE
amazon.com

TASSEL
mjtrim.com

CANVAS POUCH
kleintools.com

ALEENE'S®
LEATHER & SUEDE GLUE
ilovetocreate.com

FLEECE THROW BLANKET
amazon.com

BUTTONS
mjtrim.com

VELCRO
michaels.com

GOLD STAR STICKERS
target.com

LEATHER MATERIAL
moodfabrics.com

FELT
moodfabrics.com

GLASS VASES
jamaligarden.com

page 127

KRYLON® PREMIUM METALLIC
GOLD SPRAY PAINT
krylon.com

153

P.S.– I made this... without you!

couldn't have (inserted above "made this")

I am forever grateful to the many people who contributed throughout the process of creating this j'amazing book!

To my friend and photographer, Michael Fine: You made my vision come to life, injecting pure heart and soul. Thank you for everything.

To Jax: My better half, who allowed for this book to become a reality. There are not enough thank-yous and bouquets of flowers to shower you with.

To Amy: P.S.– we made this! I am indebted to your patience, in awe of your creative juice, dazzled by your brilliance, and blessed to have you in my life forever and ever . . . and ever.

To Babs: A million meows, hugs, friendship bracelets, love, and everything in between. You're my shining star.

To Vivian: I thank the fashion gods every day for spotting your spiked Louboutins. I knew your style, eye, and heart was a winning combo from day one.

To John: You are my rock who allowed me to roll. The sunshine in my shade. And yes . . . the cameras were rolling and they were always "getting us."

To Stacy: My soul sister. You got me before we ever got going.

To my publisher, Judith Curr, and wonderful editor, Johanna Castillo: Thank you both for your support and excitement. I'm so blessed to be working with you.

To Joey: Your home is where the art is. Thank you.

Major shout out to Janet Balis, Rachael Ray, John Cusimano, Judy Keane, Dana Olinsky, Chris Nelson, Danny DiMauro, Stefanie Syat, Maybelline, Land of Nod, Billy's Bakery, Ruschmeyer's, and The Coveteur for helping my world, my life, and my book become an amazing reality.

Last but not least, to my entire loving, supporting, out-of-this-world, fantastic blended family: Thank you for ALWAYS letting me be me and understanding my need to color outside the lines. I LOVE YOU ALL SO VERY MUCH! xo, "Belle, Nibby, Ricky Lauren, Erickie."

ABOUT THE AUTHOR

Erica Domesek, founder, creator, and author of P.S.- I made this . . . , is a distinguished DIY design and style expert living and creating in New York City. P.S.- I made this . . . inspires and encourages everyone to embrace Erica's creative motto: "I see it. I like it. I make it."

Launched as a blog in 2009, its popularity led to the release of Domesek's first book in the fall of 2010. Part designer DIY, part fashion and lifestyle inspiration guide, the book features projects inspired by iconic fashion looks, runway trends, and celebrated style mavens. A worldwide bestseller, *P.S.- I made this* has inspired millions to create.

In June 2012, Erica's prominent and influential role in the industry led her to appear as a judge on TLC's *Craft Wars*. She has also been seen crafting with Rachael Ray, Martha Stewart, and Nate Berkus, and on Fox, NBC, E! News, and CBS. Her work has been featured in publications such as *Teen Vogue, Glamour, Lucky, InStyle, Self, Vogue Italia, Seventeen,* and *The Wall Street Journal*. She has styled and designed campaigns and creative programs for international brands such as Gap, Saks Fifth Avenue, Coca-Cola, Ford, Helmut Lang, Bloomingdales, Swiss Army, Swarovski, Fossil, and Sharpie, in addition to digital collaborations with Oscar de la Renta, DKNY, Tory Burch, WhoWhatWear, Fashionista, Refinery29, DesignSponge, and more.

Visit *psimadethis.com* for more DIY projects and follow the sea of inspiration on Instagram, Twitter, Pinterest, and Facebook.

@psimadethis   @psimadethis   pinterest.com/psimadethis   facebook.com/psimadethis   psimadethis.com   youtube.com/psimadethis